Science
Level K
Student Edition-Book 1

Author
Huma Bokharey
MA Public Administration
Professional Educationist
Elementary School Founder/Principal
ILM Academy, Fremont, CA

Cover and Science Poems Illustrations
Aymun Sajid
Fine Arts
Islamabad, Pakistan

Editing and Layout
Irum Sarfaraz
MA English Literature
Language Arts Director, Publications Editor
ILM Academy
Fremont, CA

Content Consultation
Maulana Tameem Ahmadi
Imam and Principal Darul Ulum
Founder, Nur Institute, Fremont, CA
Director, Masjid al-Huda, Fremont, CA

Reshma Farooqui
BSc Science,
Director of Curriculum, MS/HS Math & Science
Ilm Academy
Fremont, CA

Special Thanks
Sapienza Educational Publishing is grateful to the faculty and students of Ilm Academy for the valuable contributions they have made to the content of the Kindergarten Science book.

Sapienza Educational Publishing is the publishing division of the ILM Academy Fremont, CA. It is committed to Islamic school education to enable Muslim educators and schools worldwide to teach sciences in the light of Al Qur'an ul Kareem and connect the students to the Creator. ILM Academy is a member of ISLA (The Islamic Schools League of America).

The translation of the Qur'anic verses are taken from the Holy Qur'an (Saheeh International) and are authenticated and deemed appropriate by our esteemed scholar of Islam, Maulana Tameem Ahmadi.

The images and the pictures in the textbooks are in the public domain and are taken from Morguefile.com. They are used according to the licensing specifications associated with free "commercial use" with permission from adminmorguefile.com. Some of the graphics are taken from Bing free images under license filter of "Free to modify, share, and use commercially".

Please note this publication contains verses from the Holy Quran and Hadith of the Prophet Muhammad (SAW). We request that extreme care be taken in the handling of the book.

D1604960

Bismillahir Rahmanir Raheem

The signs of Allah (SWT)—the existence of our Creator—are scattered throughout the cosmos like stars in the night sky. Like a precious diamond hidden from the eyes of the unworthy, the Creator wishes that He be discovered only by the worthy seekers who recognize Him through the signs He has so magnificently placed in His creation. All these signs lead to one direction and ultimately end up at a single destination—the Almighty Fashioner and Creator: Allah (SWT).

This is why for centuries Muslims have always excelled in scientific exploration and have been leading contributors to the sciences. For Muslims, there are no religious prohibitions with regards to involvement in science or its study because the religion requires them to observe, study, ponder, and reflect upon the creation around them as a religious obligation.

The Noble Qur'an states:

"We will show you Our signs in the universe and

in yourselves until you are convinced that He is the truth."

[41:53]

In this regard, I commend Sister Huma Bokharey for her efforts in publishing a primary science textbook which beautifully incorporates the relevant verses from the Noble Qur'an and prophetic traditions that correlate with the subject matter being discussed.

I have reviewed the textbook and have found it very beneficial for the spiritual nourishment of young blossoming minds. May Allah Ta'ala accept it out of His infinite mercy and make it a means of guidance for all who read it. Ameen.

Tameem Ahmadi

Fremont, CA 3/10/14

A Very Special Thanks

It is to our great advantage that we have the blessing of consulting with and benefiting from the advice and knowledge of scholars. We fall short of words with which to embody our appreciation, nor are there sufficient means by which to express our gratitude, for the blessings that Allah (SWT) has provided us in the form of our scholars and their subsequent influence upon our lives.

This project was started by the permission of Mufti Mudassir Owais. Mufti Mudassir Owais (may Allah preserve him) is the teacher and resident scholar at ICF, Islamic Center of Fremont. He currently heads numerous scholastic efforts and also serves as a counselor and mentor for all ages of both the dedicated and the casual seekers of Islamic knowledge.

The ayat ul-Qur'an and ahadeeth contained within this work have been reviewed, authenticated, and deemed appropriate by Maulana Tameem Ahmadi.

Maulana Tameem (may Allah (SWT) preserve him) is a Bay Area resident. After initially studying at San Francisco State University he went on to pursue the higher calling of sacred knowledge. Over the greater part of the next decade, Maulana Tameem engaged in a rigorous curriculum of religious knowledge, studying under some of the foremost scholars of North America, Africa, & South Asia. He is a graduate of Jamia Binoria Madrassa in Karachi, Pakistan, where he received his master's degree in Arabic and Islamic Studies.

Maulana Tameem is the Imam and Director of Masjid al-Huda in Union City, California, and the Founder of Nur Institute, dedicated to Islamic education and enrichment. He is currently the principal of Darul-Ulum, Fremont, ICF, where he teaches future-generation scholars of Islam in the esteemed Aalim Course program.

" Our Lord! Accept (this service) from us.
Verily! You are the All-Hearer, the All-Knower."
Ameen thumma Ameen
[Al-Qur'an 16:78]

Unit 1
Exploring Our World

Lesson Goals

By the end of the lesson:

1. Students will know that Allah (SWT) has created everything.
2. Students will learn about body parts.
3. Students will study the five senses.
4. Students will learn about the scientific method.
5. Students will learn about some important safety rules in science.

Our World!

This is a story about our world.

The world that we see around us every day.

You and I are part of the world that Allah (SWT) has created.

Everything around us are signs from Allah (SWT).

It is through the study of science that you will learn how Allah (SWT) has created everything.

Allah (SWT) has created this entire universe without the use of any materials or tools. Allah (SWT) does not need anything to make whatever He wants to do.

		Yes	No
Would you like to build something?			
Do you think you can do it without any materials?			
Do you think it is possible?			

Use your Lego blocks to make a toy.

We cannot make anything without materials.

But Allah (SWT) does not need any tools or materials to create anything.

Only Allah (SWT) can do that. Because He is the Creator.

Circle everything created by Allah (SWT). Put an X on everything that is man-made.

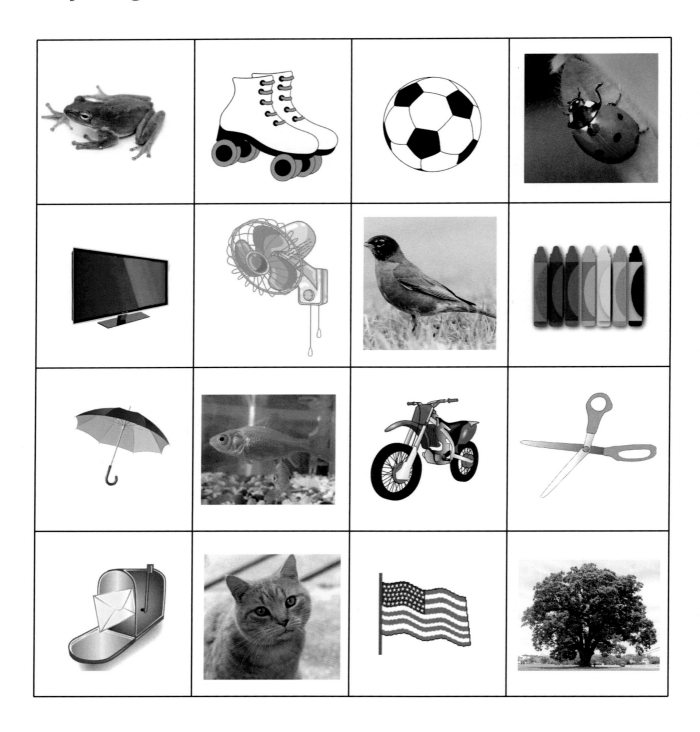

What is created by Allah (SWT)?

The sky is created by Allah (SWT).

Color the sky blue.

Animals are created by Allah (SWT).

Color the horse brown.

The plants are created by Allah (SWT)

Color the flowers and the leaves.

A scientist is someone who studies the creations of Allah (SWT). There are many different types of scientists in the world. They all study different things in order to learn more about them.

The weatherman is a scientist who tells us whether it will rain or not.

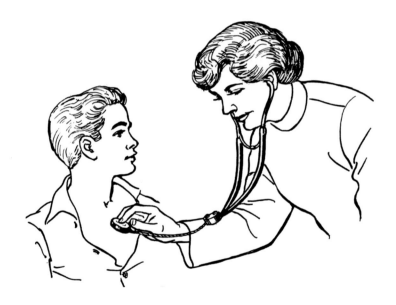

A doctor is a scientist who tells us why we are feeling ill.

Zoologists are scientists who study animals.

Remember, Allah (SWT) created everything. He wants us to study His creations to understand them. When we know His creations, we know Him.

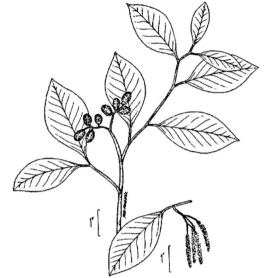

A botanist is a scientist who studies plants and flowers.

An astronomer is a scientist who studies the stars, the sun, and the moon.

A geologist is a scientist who studies the earth and the rocks.

Allah (SWT) Made Me

(To the Tune of 'Twinkle Twinkle, Little Star')

Allah Allah,

You made me

Allah Allah,

You made the sea

All the mountains and the hills

The vast blue sky

So blue and high

14

The tiniest animal

And the largest too

All created by none but You

All created by none but You

Allah Allah,

You made me

Allah Allah,

You made the sea

Irum Sarfaraz

Can you connect the right body part to the name?

Head

Face

Fingers

Shoulder

Hand

Arm

Leg

Foot

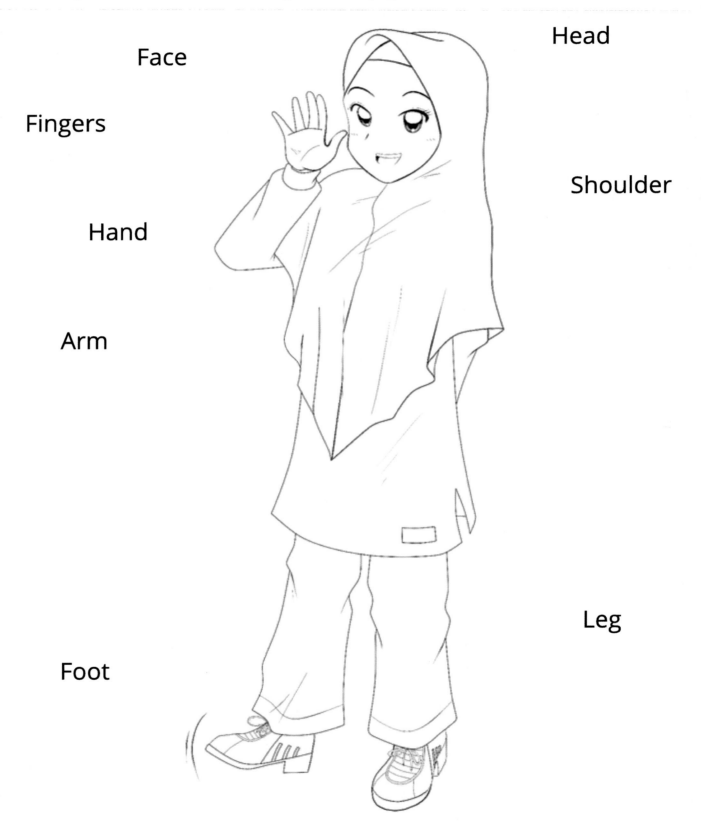

Sense of Sight

We have our **eyes** that helps us see all the wonderful colors and images.

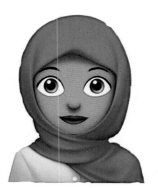

Activity:

	Yes	No
Close your eyes and look outside. Are you able to see anything?		
Open your eyes and look outside. Are you able to see anything?		

On your sketch pad, draw some of the things you are able to see with your eyes open.

Sense of Smell

Our **nose** helps us to smell. Our nose tells us whether we like the smell or don't like it.

Activity:

Look at the items below. Do you think that would be a good smell or a bad smell? Color the right box.

	Good Smell	Bad Smell
Trash		
Flower Bunch		
Worn Socks		
Cup-Cakes 		

Sense of Taste

Our **tongue** helps us to taste delicious food. Our tongue tells us whether we are eating candy or cheese.

Activity:

Connect the picture of the food to how you think it tastes. How many things were you able to guess correctly?

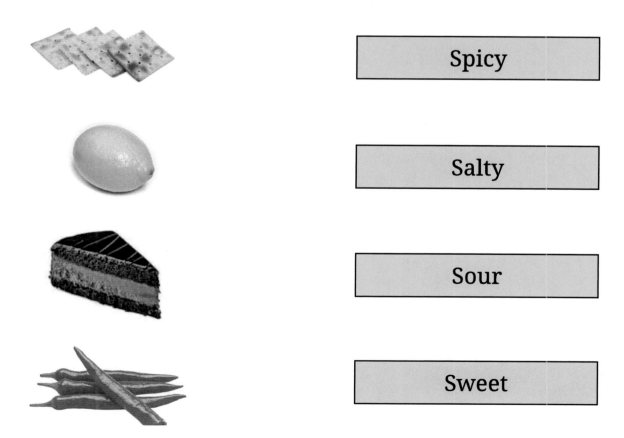

	Spicy

	Salty

	Sour

	Sweet

Sense of Hearing

Our **ears** help us hear sounds. We use our ears to understand other people talking. Our ears tell us hear the pitter-patter of the rain and the roar of thunder.

Activity:

Connect the sound to the picture. How many things were you able to guess correctly?

Sense of Touch

Our **skin** help us feel if something hot or cold, or smooth or rough. Have you ever touched a cat? It is your sense of touch that tells you how its fur feels.

Activity:

Find Things That Feel....	Draw Them Here...
SOFT	
HARD	
ROUGH	
SMOOTH	

Mark an X in the correct senses you would use to enjoy all of the things below.

ice cream cone					
flower					
cat					
teacher					
trash can					
storm					

A scientist is using all five senses.

Name and label each sense and the body part.

Match the tools to the word.

Thermometer

Microscope

Balance Scale

Magnifying Glass

Magnets

Food Scale

Ruler

Measuring Cup

Let's do an activity to help you understand the **scientific method.**

Materials:

Disposable Bowl

Dropper

Spoon

Vinegar

Baking Soda

Method:

Your teacher will place 10 drops of vinegar in the disposable bowl with the help of a dropper. Your teacher will add a teaspoon of baking soda to the vinegar.

Now use your senses to **observe.**

What do you...

See

Hear

Smell

25

 Look around you. Draw what you **observe.**

On your desk.

In your classroom.

 Ask a question.

Why, how, where, who, what, when (question words).

Ask questions about the picture. Share your questions with the rest of the class in circle time. Color the picture.

 Make an intelligent guess for the questions you have. This is called hypothesis.

Activity:

What do you think will happen to these things if you blow on them? Put an x in your intelligent guess.

		Will Move	**Will Not Move**
Feather			
Balloon			
Brick			
Pencil			

Test your hypothesis. Blow on each item. Put and X in the correct box for each item.

		Moved	Did Not Move
Feather			
Balloon			
Brick			
Pencil			

Analyze t**he Result**. See if your experiment gave the results that support your hypothesis. Why and why not?

We do experiments in a lab.

Which ice-cubes will melt faster? Make an intelligent guess.

What You Need:

3 Paper Cups   9 Ice Cubes   Plain Water

What To Do:
1. Take a cup and write A on it.
2. Take the other cup and mark it B.
3. Take the third cup and mark it C.
4. Put 1 ice cube in cup A.
5. Put 3 ice cubes in cup B.
6. Put 5 ice cubes in cup C.
7. Fill each cup halfway with plain water.
8. Leave the cups for 15 minutes.

Intelligent Guess:

Which ice cubes do you think will melt faster? Color the box.

A	B	C

Observation:

After 15 minutes, look inside the three cups closely. Which ice cubes have melted the most?

A	B	C

Result of Experiment:

The cubes in cup _____ melted the most. The cubes in cup_____ did not melt much. The cubes in cup_____ were slowest to melt.

Physical Science

Lesson Goals

By the end of the lesson:

1. Students will learn about matter and its states.
2. Students will know what are atoms and molecules.
3. Students will learn about force and different forms of force.
4. Students will learn about density.
5. Students will learn about magnets.
6. Students will understand that light is also a a form of energy.

What is EVERYTHING in the universe made of?

Everything is Matter.

Everything is matter. Planet Earth is matter.

Can you think of something else?

Look outside, where do you find matter?

Matter –Matter Everywhere

Look at yourself. Do you take up space?

If you sit on a chair can someone else come and sit on that chair?

Are you matter?

      Yes   No

Everything that has mass and takes up space is matter. People, water, rocks, air, even moon and stars are examples of matter. Color the pictures of matter.

Matter is the stuff everything is made of. Different kinds of matter are known by their **mass**.

Mass is the amount of matter or stuff that makes up an object.

Look at the picture of a balloon and a brick. Remember your activity in chapter one.

Balloon moved.   Brick did not move.

A balloon has less mass.   Brick has more mass.

Balloon is light.   Brick is heavy.

When you blew on balloon , it moved because it has less mass and is **lighter** than a brick.

When you blew on the brick it did not move because it has more mass and it is **heavier** than the balloon.

Quiz: Discuss and Complete the following sentences.

1. Mass is the amount of _____ in an object.

2. Color the one with more mass.

    light   heavy

3. Circle the one with less mass.

a bowling ball   a beach ball

 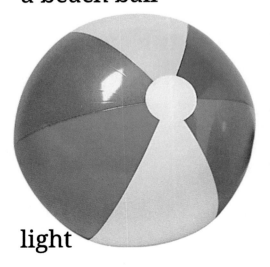

    heavy   light

36

Volume is how much space something takes up. Look at the two glasses. One is a small glass and one is a big glass.

Fill the small glass with water.

Now pour the small glass water into the big glass.

You will see that the amount of water that filled the small glass is not enough to fill the big glass.

1. Circle the glass that has more space and more volume?

2. Put an X on the glass that has less space and less volume?

The Matter Song

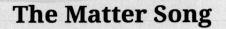

(To the Tune of 'Are You Sleeping')

It is matter, is it matter

How do you know?

How do you know?

First you find its volume

First you find its volume

You know it takes up space

You know it takes up space

It is matter, is it matter

How do you know?

How do you know?

38

Next you find its mass
Next you find its mass
You know it's light
You know it's heavy

I am matter, you are matter
Everywhere we see
Everywhere we see

Allah made the matter
Water and the air
For you and me
For you and me!
(Alhumdullilah)

Huma Bokharey

39

Remember, Volume is the amount of space something takes.

A long time ago, a man named Archimedes lived in a country called Greece. He loved Math and numbers. One day Archimedes decided to take a bath. He filled the tub with water and sat down in the tub. He saw the water level in the tub rise. He knew at that time that he discovered something important. He found a way to tell how much space an object takes up.

He got so excited and jumped out of the tub and forgot to put on his clothes and ran down the street yelling "Eureka" in Greek language meaning "I found it".

Matter is made of very tiny particles called **atom**.

Just like you can take the small Lego blocks and connect them together to make a larger object.

Do you like to play with Lego blocks?

Join the Lego blocks together to make a bigger toy.

Just like Lego blocks , Atoms join together to make matter.

Look at the glass jug. The jug is matter.

Many small atoms that you can not see make the jug.

tiny atom

Make the jug with tiny atoms.

41

Molecules

When two or more atoms come together, they make a **Molecule**. Molecules make up everything.

They even make your skin, hair, teeth, leaves, flower, fruit, and water that you drink.

Just like Lego blocks, they are the building blocks of nature.

The water that you drink is made of molecules.

One water molecule has two atoms of Hydrogen and one atom of oxygen.

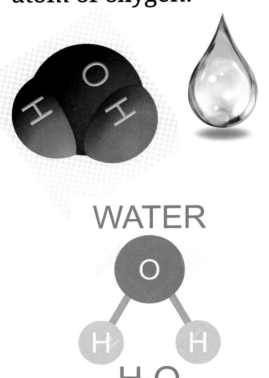

WATER

H_2O

Fill the water bottle with water molecules.

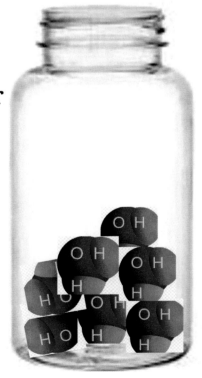

Activity:

Can you separate the following objects into groups of same class of matter? What objects go together?

Circle the object that belongs to the same group as A.

Put an X on the object that belongs to the same group as B.

Put a ✓ on the object that belongs to the same group as C.

A	Water	**Pencil**	**Juice**
B	**Spoon**	**Smoke**	**Fog**
C	**Air** [AIR]	**Milk**	**Table**

Question: Which item out of the three changes shape?

Materials:

1 Balloon Half Blown

1 Jug of Water

1 Empty Bowl

1 Piece of Wood

Make a hypothesis.

Hypothesis: I think this item will change shape.

Balloon   Wood   Water

Method:

1. Hold the balloon in your hand and try to twist it (the teacher will demonstrate how). You will notice that the shape of the balloon will change as you put pressure on it.

2. Transfer the water from the bowl into the empty cup. Notice how the water changes its shape.

3. Try and twist the piece of wood. Move it from one place to another. You will notice that the piece of wood doesn't change its shape.

Was your prediction correct? What did you find out?

Result: Mark an x on the item that changed shape.

We will do this simple experiment to see how matter changes form by heat.

Materials: 4 Ice-cubes, Ice-cube Tray, Glass Measuring Cup

Method:

1. Place the 4 ice-cubes in the measuring cup.

What form of matter are the ice-cubes?

Solid	Liquid	Gas

2. Your teacher will heat the ice-cubes in the microwave. Do you see the steam rising from the cup?

What form of matter have the ice-cubes turned into?

Solid	Liquid	Gas

3. Look inside the cup.
What happened to the ice-cubes?

What form of matter have they turned into?

Solid	Liquid	Gas

4. Pour the water back in the ice-cube tray. Put it in the freezer.

What form of matter will this matter turn into?

Solid	Liquid	Gas

Density measures the mass of a matter compared to its volume. The lighter the object is, the lower is the density.

The heavier the object is, the higher the density.

Remember, if an object is less dense than water it will float. If an object is more dense than water it will sink.

Let's Try: The following items are all about the same size. Which of these items are more dense than water and will sink in the cup of water?

Put one object at a time in the water bowl. Does the object sink or float (stays at the surface of the water).

keys   Cork   pencil   Rubber duck   Golf ball   water bowl

Circle the objects that will sink because of their density.

Sink and Float

Question: Which object do you think will sink or float?

Materials: Foam Ball, Rubber Duck, Coin, Rock, Bowl of Water.

Mark an X in the box.

	Objects	Sink	Float
Foam Ball			
Rubber Duck			
Rock			
Coin			

Method:

1. Place all the four objects in the bowl of water one by one.

2. Looks carefully and see which objects float and which do not.

How correct were your answers?

Discuss why things float and why they sink.

Allah (SWT) has created us and the whole world in perfect order. Remember, in the previous lesson you learned about the body parts that Allah (SWT) has given to us.

Your body parts help you move.

When you move, you are not **still.**

You are not at rest. When an

object is not still, it is in **motion.**

What do you see in this picture? Color the picture.

Can you move your body? Let's try.

Can you jump? Jump four times then

stop.

Can you run? Run a circle then stop.

Can you bend?

Put your hands up, bend down and touch your toes.

We are thankful to Allah (SWT) for the gifts He has given to us.

Movement Song

(To the Tune of 'Hokey Pokey')

When I move my legs
They make me run and walk
When I move my hands,
They help me grab and hold
I like to move, I like to swing

When I move my mouth
It makes me eat and talk
When I move my head
I can turn around,
Swing around

50

I thank my Allah for the gifts I got
I thank my Allah for the gifts I got

I can go up and down
I can swing around
I can see the world
And know the world
I thank my Allah for the gifts I got

Huma Bokharey

Remember, you learned all about matter and about your body parts that Allah (SWT) has given to you.

Your feet help you move from one place to another.

Your hands help you move things around.

A monkey swings tree to tree.

It moves from one tree to

another by swinging.

When something changes place or position, it moves. This is called **movement.** When something moves it changes **position** and it is not **still**.

Write a movement word for each movement in the picture.

Words: **run**   **fly**   **jump**

_____   _____   _____

Motion is a change in position.

Do you wonder what types of things can move?

Look at the two pictures below and tell which one can move by itself.

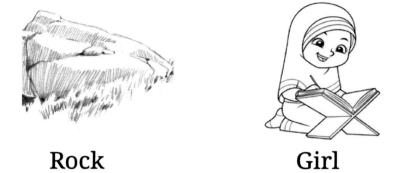

Rock   Girl

Color the one that can move by itself.

Yes! You are right!

The girl can move by herself because Allah (SWT) has given us the gift of movement. Even our eyelids are moving all the time when we blink. A rock cannot move on its own. Someone has to move the rock.

Activity: Make it Move

Objects	How Can You Make Them Move?
Ball	
Marble	
Wooden Block	

Do you wonder how things move?

53

Movement is all around us. The birds are flying, the cars are moving, the ball is falling back to the ground, the earth, the sun, and the moon all are moving.

Things move in many different ways.

Look at the rocket
It moves straight up.

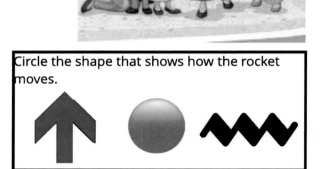

Circle the shape that shows how the rocket moves.

A wheel moves
round and round.

Circle the shape that shows how the wheel moves.

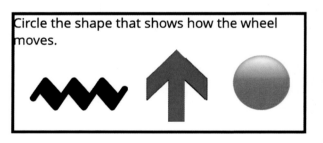

A bike moves zigzag
on this path.

Circle the shape that shows how the bike moves.

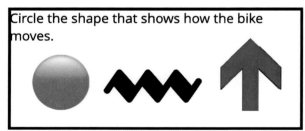

Technology Connect:

Can objects move on their own? If you tell a book to move can it move?

Directions of Movement

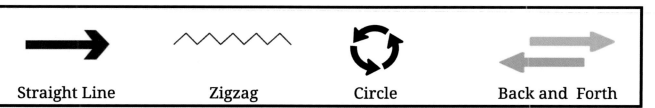

Straight Line   Zigzag   Circle   Back and Forth

The child blows on the pinwheel.

It moves in a circle.

Put an X on pictures that move in a circle.

A girl swings.

The swing moves back and forth.

Mark X on the picture that move back and forth.

Lesson Review:

Fill in the circle next to the answer.

The swing moves back

and forth because...

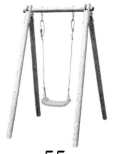

- ◯ someone pushes it.
- ◯ it moves by itself.
- ◯ of a sound.

Movement Chart

Question: Do you wonder different ways that you can make an object move?

Hypothesis: We think that we can move objects in many different ways.

Let's **Investigate**

Process: Let's make a chart of objects that we can move. We are going to do this by finding different objects in the room.

Materials: Go around the room to find four objects that you can move. Some examples are given find some more objects.

Experiment: Circle all the movements that you used to move the object.

Object	Push	Pull
Ball	Kick	Lift
	Roll	Drag
	Bump	Slide
	Drop	Walk
	Run	Bounce

Results: All objects can be moved around by using many different forces. If you move a backpack with wheels you pull it to move it. You are applying force to move the bag.

Push

Which items can you push easily?

Materials:

1 Straw, 1 Dead Leaf or Cotton Ball, 1 Key

Hypothesis:

Which items will be pushed easily.

Method:

1. Use the straw to blow on the cotton ball and the quarter.

Make an X on the object that moved.

2. Now blow on the key and the leaf.

Make an X on the object that moved.

Result:

Was your prediction correct? Make an X on the objects that moved.

How Things Move—Push and Pull

Scientists find out that push and pull are forces that make things move.

A child's push can move the shopping cart.

A baby's pull can move the wagon.

Circle the correct answer.

1. What is the force that moves the shopping cart?

   PUSH   **PULL**

1. What is the force that moves the wagon?

   PUSH   **PULL**

Explore: Place a pencil at the corner of the table. Slowly push the pencil with one finger to the center of the table.

When you push the pencil you use the force through your finger.

Sort the objects by push or pull.

Put an X for each object.

Object	Push	Push & Pull	Pull

Maya Likes to Swing

Maya is a little two year old girl. She loves to play in her Grandma's (Nano) backyard.

One day as she came to her Nano's house. She ran into the backyard.

Her favorite playtime is on the swings.

Maya ran and sat on the swing.

"Push Nano, push harder!" said Maya.

Maya's Nano gave her a gentle push, the swing moved slowly.

"Faster, Nano, faster!" yelled Maya.

Maya's grandma moved back.
She put her hands in front of her
and gave Maya a BIG push.

"Wheeeee!" screamed Maya. "Not so hard Nano!
Slowly please!
Stop the swing!"

 Maya's Nano pulled the swing back to slow it down.

The swing stopped moving.

Maya had so much fun!

1. What is Maya's favorite place to play in the story?

     Zoo   Toy store   Backyard

2. Maya's Nano gave her a little push. What happened?

    a) She barely moved   b) She stopped moving

    c) She moved very fast

3. Maya's Nano gave her a big push. What happened?

    a) She went faster.   b) She went slower.

    c) She spun in a circle.

4. Maya wanted to stop. What did her Nano do?

    a) Nano told the swing to stop.

    b) Nano pulled the swing back.

Can you move things without using a physical force?

Materials:

Shoe Box 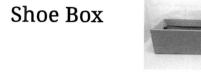 Magnet

Piece of Cloth  Piece of Thread

Paper Clip

Procedure:

1. Get a shoe box, hold it upside down.

2. Now insert a magnet inside the box and hold it with your hand against the top of the box from inside.

3. With your left hand place a paper clip on top of the box.

4. Move the magnet with your right hand slowly.

5. Do you see the paper clip moving and following the magnet all around?

Result:

What did you observe?

You observed that the paper clip is ATTRACTED to the magnet. Try to move a penny, dime, and a nail.

Gravity!

(To the Tune of 'Wheels On the Bus')

Gravity, gravity
All around
All around
All around
Gravity, gravity all around
It keeps us in our place

When I throw a ball up high
Ball up high,
Ball up high
It comes falling back to me
Doesn't fly away

When I jump up

Really High

High above,

High above,

Gravity pulls me down below,

Down below

Down below

Gravity pulls me

Down below

Pulls me down

Pulls me down

Gravity pulls me down below

It's a force that I can't see

Huma Bokharey

Will these objects be attracted to the magnet?
Circle Yes or No for each object.

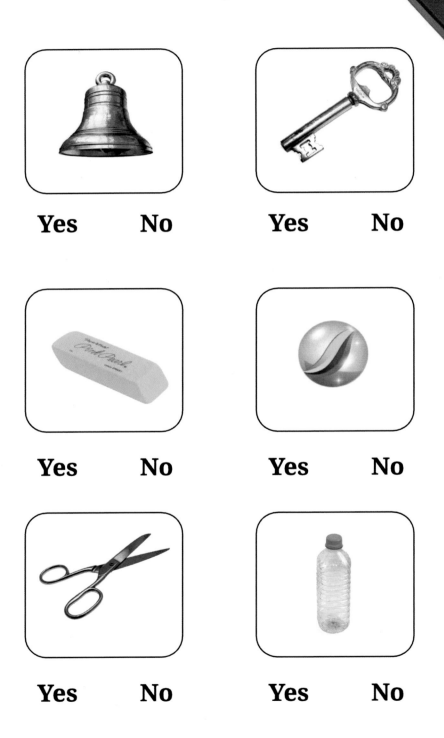

Yes   No   Yes   No

Yes   No   Yes   No

Yes   No   Yes   No

Who Discovered Gravity?

Long time ago there was a scientist name Isaac Newton. One day, Isaac was sitting outside under an apple tree. He saw an apple fall from the tree. It made him wonder!

Why did the apple fall straight to Earth? Why didn't it go up to the sky?

Suddenly, Isaac knew something. The Earth must pull on the apple! Isaac Newton called this force of pull GRAVITY.

It was a huge discovery in the year 1665-1667.

Look at the apple tree.

What causes the apple to fall to the ground?

What is happening to Mr. Newton in the picture?

Newton was the first scientist to discover a force called Gravity that causes the apple to fall to the ground. Gravity acts on an object to make it move.

Can you walk on the earth without the force of gravity? Let's discuss: Why or Why not!

Does gravity make the waterfall

go up or down?

Up   Down

The water flows down because of the force of pull of the gravity. You do not see this force but it is all around us.

The force of gravity enables us to walk, run, and live on earth.

Q.1. Ahmed is closing the door. Is Ahmed using a *pushing force* or a *pulling force* to close the door?

a) pushing force

b) pulling force

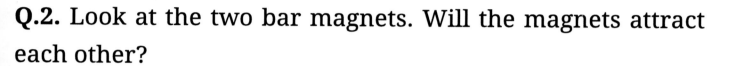

Q.2. Look at the two bar magnets. Will the magnets attract each other?

a)   Yes

b) No

Q.3. Dad is mowing the grass. How can he move the lawn mower to go faster?

a) push gently

b) push harder

Magnets!

(To the Tune of 'Round the Mulberry Bush')

A magnet can

Push and pull

Push and pull

Push and pull

A magnet can push n pull

Metals all around

A magnet can

Attract and repel

Attract and repel

Attract and repel

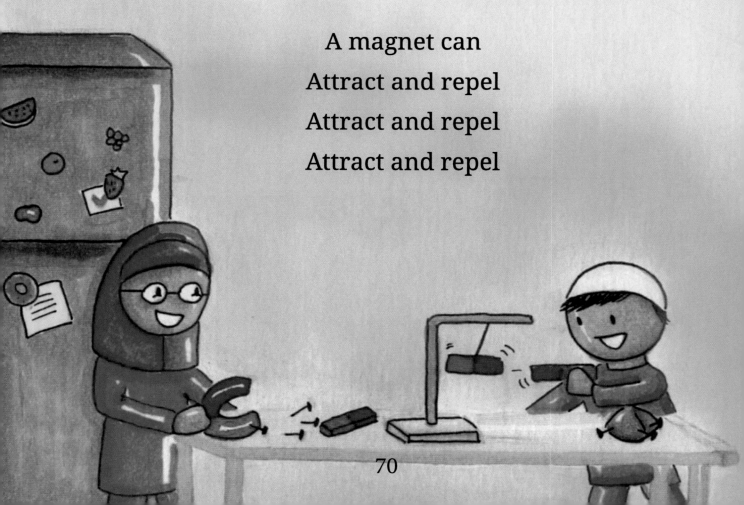

A magnet can
Attract and repel
Materials all around

Allah gave us
Ores and lodestone
Ores and lodestone
Ores and lodestone
Allah gave us ores and lodestone
To use on planet Earth

Huma Bokharey

In the previous lesson you learned how Allah (SWT) has made it possible for us to move and live on the planet Earth.

We are thankful to Allah (SWT) for all the gifts He has given us.

Let us discuss this picture.

What do you see?

How does this picture make you feel?

What colors do you see?

What might these colors mean?

How many light bulbs would you use to light up the sky?

Allah (SWT) has created the Sun. Sun is a very important source of energy. Without sun there can be no life for animals, people , and plants on the planet Earth.

Sun comes out in the morning to give us the light and energy.

The moon and stars shine at night time to give us light in the dark.

Draw the Natural light source for the day and night.

Just like you plants need to be protected from the sun heat. People use different shade covers to protect the plants.

Activity:

Circle all items that you need to protect yourself from the heat of the sun.

Now you know that we get heat from the sun. The sun radiates heat and make things very warm.

Q. What happens to the chocolate in the sun?

Hypothesis: I think my chocolate will _____.

Materials: two chocolate bars   two foil tray   sun

Procedure:

1. Place one chocolate in each foil tray.

2. Place one foil tray directly under the sun.

3. Place second foil tray under the shade.

4. Leave the foil trays out for one hour.

5. Check the trays and discuss what happened and why.

Result: Was your hypothesis correct?   yes   no

Draw a picture to show what happened.

Chocolate Bar	Chocolate Bar in the Sun	Chocolate Bar in the Shade

Now you know that sunlight warms the Earth's surface and all the objects on the earth that are under the sun.

People build many different structures to protect themselves and their animals from the sun's heat.

They want to be in the shade to protect themselves from the direct sunlight.

Build a shade for your toy duck.

Artificial Light

The artificial light is the man –made light.

It is NOT natural light.

What are some things that you use to see in the dark when you have no light?

Draw a line from the word to the picture.

Table Lamp

Candles

Flashlight

Light Bulb

Can you think of some more sources of artificial light?

Look at the objects in the box.

What do we do with the different items in the box?

Write the names of the items you can use on a hot sunny day.

_____   _____   _____

Discuss what items you can use on a cold cloudy day.

_____   _____   _____

Discuss what items you can use on a rainy day.

_____   _____   _____

Understand the effect of light wind/strong wind on some material.

Material:

1. Hand fan

2. Feather

3. Paper

4. Small Toy

5. Big Toy

Materials:

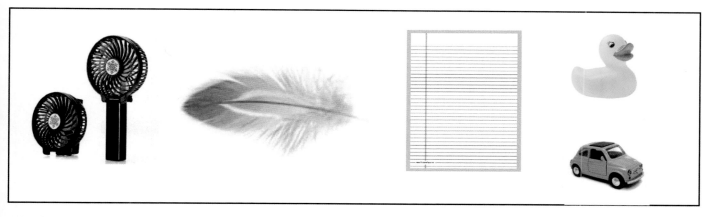

Step 1. Work with a friend. Hold an object in front of the fan while it is on low.

Tell your friend what happened to the object.

Step 2: Repeat step 1 with the fan on high.

Observe what happened. Which object moved and which object didn't move, and why.

The weather reporter gives the weather forecast. He forecasts the weather daily either for ten days or for more than ten days.

Today you are the weather reporter and will report the weather to the class.

Weekly Weather Chart

	Monday	Tuesday	Wednesday	Thursday

Concepts - Standards	Chapter #
K-ESS3-1 Use a model to represent the relationship between the needs of different plants and animals (including humans) and the places they live. [Clarification Statement: Examples of relationships could include that deer eat buds and leaves; therefore, they usually live in forested areas; and, grasses need sunlight so they often grow in meadows. Plants, animals, and their surroundings make up a system.	Ch-9,10,15
K-LS1-1 Examples of patterns could include that animals need to take in food but plants do not; the different kinds of food needed by different types of animals; the requirement of plants to have light; and, that all living things need water.]	Ch-11
K-ESS3-3 Communicate solutions that will reduce the impact of humans on the land, water, air, and/or other living things in the local environment. Examples of human impact on the land could include cutting trees to produce paper and using resources to produce bottles. Examples of solutions could include reusing paper and recycling cans and bottles. **Plant roots break the ground.** **Plants look different with or without sufficient water.** **The places where different plants and animals live have particular water features, soil, weather, etc. in the area.**	Ch-11,12
Students identify patterns in the organized data, including that: i. All animals eat food. 1. Some animals eat plants. 2. Some animals eat other animals. 3. Some animals eat both plants and animals. 4. No animals do not eat food. ii. All animals drink water. iii. Plants cannot live or grow if there is no water. iv. Plants cannot live or grow if there is no light.	Ch-15
Students describe* that the patterns they identified in the data provide evidence that: iii. Plants need light and water to live and grow. ii. Animals need food and water to live and grow. iii. Animals get their food from plants, other animals, or both.	Ch-15

ESS2.D: Weather and Climate
Weather is the combination of sunlight, wind, snow or rain, and temperature in a particular region at a particular time. People measure these conditions to describe and record the weather and to notice patterns over time. With guidance, students organize data from given observations (firsthand or from media) about local weather conditions using graphical displays (e.g., pictures, charts). The weather condition data include:
i̟ The number of sunny, cloudy, rainy, windy, cool, or warm days.
ii. The relative temperature at various times of the day (e.g., cooler in the morning, warmer during the day, cooler at night).
2 Identifying relationships
Students identify and describe* patterns in the organized data, including:
   i.   The relative number of days of different types of weather conditions in a month.
   ii.   The change in the relative temperature over the course of a day.
	Ch-19

3 Interpreting data
Students describe* and share that:
   i.   Certain months have more days of some kinds of weather than do other months (e.g., some months have more hot days, some have more rainy days).
   ii.   The differences in relative temperature over the course of a day (e.g., between early morning and the afternoon, between one day and another) are directly related to the time of day.
	Ch-10,19

ESS2.E: Biogeology • Plants and animals can change their environment.	Ch-11
ESS3.C: Human Impacts on Earth Systems Things that people do to live comfortably can affect the world around them. But they can make choices that reduce their impacts on the land, water, air, and other living things.) Students make a claim to be supported about a phenomenon. In their claim, students include the idea that plants and animals (including humans) can change the environment to meet their needs.	Ch-13

2 Identifying scientific evidence
Students identify and describe* the given evidence to support the claim, including:
   i.   Examples of plants changing their environments (e.g., plant roots lifting sidewalks).
   ii.   Examples of animals (including humans) changing their environments (e.g., ants building an ant hill, humans clearing land to build houses, birds building a nest, squirrels digging holes to hide food).
	Ch-11,12,15

82

iii.	Examples of plant and animal needs (e.g., shelter, food, room to grow).	

4 Reasoning and synthesis
Students support the claim and present an argument by logically connecting various needs of plants and animals to evidence about how plants/animals change their environments to meet their needs.
Students include:
  i.   Examples of how plants affect other parts of their systems by changing their environments to meet their needs (e.g., roots push soil aside as they grow to better absorb water).
  ii.   Examples of how animals affect other parts of their systems by changing their environments to meet their needs (e.g., ants, birds, rabbits, and humans use natural materials to build shelter; some animals store food for winter).
	Ch-12,13,19

ESS3.A: Natural Resources
• Living things need water, air, and resources from the land, and they live in places that have the things they need. Humans use natural resources for everything they do. From the given model (e.g., representation, diagram, drawing, physical replica, diorama, dramatization, storyboard) of a phenomenon involving the needs of living things and their environments, students identify and describe* the components that are relevant to their representations, including:
  i.   Different plants and animals (including humans).
  ii.   The places where the different plants and animals live.
  iii. The things that <u>plants</u> and animals need (e.g., water, air, and land resources such as wood, soil, and rocks).
	Ch-11,12

Relationships a Students use the given model to represent and describe* relationships between the components,
including:
  i.   The relationships between the different plants and animals and the materials they need to survive (e.g., fish need water to swim, deer need buds and leaves to eat, plants need water and sunlight to grow).
  ii.   The relationships between places where different plants and animals live and the resources those places provide.
  iii. The relationships between specific plants and animals and where they live (e.g., fish live in water environments, deer live in forests where there are buds and leaves, rabbits live in fields and woods where there is <u>grass</u> to eat and space for burrows for homes, plants live in sunny and moist areas, humans
	Ch-11,12,13,15

get resources from nature [e.g., building materials from trees to help them live where they want to live]).	
3 Connections a. Students use the given model to represent and describe*, including: i. Students use the given model to describe* the pattern of how the needs of different plants and animals are met by the various places in which they live (e.g., plants need sunlight so they are found in places that have sunlight; fish swim in water so they live in lakes, rivers, ponds, and oceans; deer eat buds and leaves so they live in the forest). ii. Students use the given model to describe* that plants and animals, the places in which they live, and the resources found in those places are each part of a system, and that these parts of systems work together and allow living things to meet their needs.	Ch-12,13
ESS3.C: Human Impacts on Earth Systems • Things that people do to live comfortably can affect the world around them. But they can make choices that reduce their impacts on the land, water, air, and other living things	Ch-13

ETS1.B: Developing Possible Solutions
• Designs can be conveyed through sketches, drawings, or physical models. These representations are useful in communicating ideas for a problem's solutions to other people.
 	
Students use prior experiences and observations to describe* information about:
    i. How people affect the land, water, air, and/or other living things in the local environment in positive and negative ways.
    ii. Solutions that reduce the negative effects of humans on the local environment.
B Students communicate information about solutions that reduce the negative effects of humans on the local environment, including:
    i. Examples of things that people do to live comfortably and how those things can cause changes to the land,
	Ch-13,14

water, air, and/or living things in the local environment. ii. Examples of choices that people can make to reduce negative impacts and the effect those choices have on the local environment. Students communicate the information about solutions with others in oral and/or written form (which include using models and/or drawings. **Think of an idea to help the planet earth.**	
K-PS3-1. Make observations to determine the effect of sunlight on Earth's surface. [Clarification Statement: Examples of Earth's surface could include sand, soil, rocks, and water.]	Ch-10,13
K-PS3-2. Use tools and materials provided to design and build a structure that will reduce the warming effect of sunlight on Earth's surface.* [Clarification Statement: Examples of structures could include umbrellas, canopies, and tents that minimize the warming effect of the sun.]	Ch-9,10
K-ESS3-2. Ask questions to obtain information about the purpose of weather forecasting to prepare for, and respond to, severe weather.* [Clarification Statement: Emphasis is on local forms of severe weather.]	Ch-9,10
K-2-ETS1-1. Ask questions, make observations, and gather information about a situation people want to change to define a simple problem that can be solved through the development of a new or improved object or tool.	Ch-16
K-PS3-1 Energy **PS3.B: Conservation of Energy and Energy Transfer** • **Sunlight warms Earth's surface.** From the given investigation plan, students describe* (with guidance) the phenomenon under investigation, which includes the following idea: sunlight warms the Earth's surface. B Students describe* (with guidance) the purpose of the investigation, which includes determining the effect of sunlight on Earth materials by identifying patterns of relative warmth of materials in sunlight and shade (e.g., sand, soil, rocks, water).	Ch-9,10,13
PS3.B: Conservation of Energy and Energy Transfer • **Sunlight warms Earth's surface.**	Ch-9,10,13

ESS2.D: Weather and Climate Weather is the combination of sunlight, wind, snow or rain, and temperature in a particular region at a particular time. People measure these conditions to describe and record the weather and to notice patterns over time. With guidance, students organize data from given observations (firsthand or from media) about local weather conditions using graphical displays (e.g., pictures, charts). The weather condition data include: i. The number of sunny, cloudy, rainy, windy, cool, or warm days. ii. The relative temperature at various times of the day (e.g., cooler in the morning, warmer during the day, cooler at night). **2 Identifying relationships** Students identify and describe* patterns in the organized data, including: 　i. The relative number of days of different types of weather conditions in a month. 　ii. The change in the relative temperature over the course of a day.	Ch-19
3 Interpreting data Students describe* and share that: 　i. Certain months have more days of some kinds of weather than do other months (e.g., some months have more hot days, some have more rainy days). 　ii. The differences in relative temperature over the course of a day (e.g., between early morning and the afternoon, between one day and another) are directly related to the time of day.	Ch-10,19
ESS2.E: Biogeology • Plants and animals can change their environment.	Ch-11
ESS3.C: Human Impacts on Earth Systems Things that people do to live comfortably can affect the world around them. But they can make choices that reduce their impacts on the land, water, air, and other living things.) Students make a claim to be supported about a phenomenon. In their claim, students include the idea that plants and animals (including humans) can change the environment to meet their needs.	Ch-13
2 Identifying scientific evidence Students identify and describe* the given evidence to support the claim, including: 　i. Examples of plants changing their environments (e.g., plant roots lifting sidewalks). 　ii. Examples of animals (including humans) changing their environments (e.g., ants building an ant hill, humans clearing land to build houses, birds building a nest, squirrels digging holes to hide food).	Ch-11,12,15

From the given investigation plan, students describe* (with guidance) the phenomenon under investigation, which includes the following idea: sunlight warms the Earth's surface. b Students describe* (with guidance) the purpose of the investigation, which includes determining the effect of sunlight on Earth materials by identifying patterns of relative warmth of materials in sunlight and shade (e.g., sand, soil, rocks, water).	

2 Identifying the evidence to address the purpose of the investigation
   a. Based on the given investigation plan, students describe* (with guidance) the evidence that will result from the investigation, including observations of the relative warmth of materials in the presence and absence of sunlight (i.e., qualitative measures of temperature: e.g., hotter, warmer, colder).
   b. Students describe* how the observations they make connect to the purpose of the investigation.
	Ch-9

3 Planning the investigation
Based on the given investigation plan, students describe* (with guidance):
   i.   The materials on the Earth's surface to be investigated (e.g., dirt, sand, rocks, water, grass).
   ii.   How the relative warmth of the materials will be observed and recorded.
	Ch-13,14

PS3.B: Conservation of Energy and Energy Transfer
☐ Sunlight warms Earth's surface.
   a.   Students use given scientific information about sunlight's warming effect on the Earth's surface to collaboratively design and build a structure that reduces warming caused by the sun.
  b. With support, students individually describe*:
i.   The problem.
ii.   The design solution.
iii.   In what way the design solution uses the given scientific information.
 	
2   Describing* specific features of the design solution, including quantification when appropriate
   a.   Students describe* that the structure is expected to reduce warming for a designated area by providing shade.
   b.   Students use only the given materials and tools when building the structure.
3.   Evaluating potential solutions
  a. Students describe* whether the structure meets the expectations in terms of cause (structure blocks sunlight) and effect (less warming of the surface).
	Ch-9,10

ESS2.D: Weather and Climate • Weather is the combination of sunlight, wind, snow or rain, and temperature in a particular region at a particular time. People measure these conditions to describe and record the weather and to notice patterns over time. With guidance, students organize data from given observations (firsthand or from media) about local weather conditions using graphical displays (e.g., pictures, charts). The weather condition data include: i. The number of sunny, cloudy, rainy, windy, cool, or warm days. ii. The relative temperature at various times of the day (e.g., cooler in the morning, warmer during the day, cooler at night).	Ch-10

2 Identifying relationships
Students identify and describe* patterns in the organized data, including:
    i.   The relative number of days of different types of weather conditions in a month.
    ii.   The change in the relative temperature over the course of a day.
3 Interpreting data
Students describe* and share that:
    i.   Certain months have more days of some kinds of weather than do other months (e.g., some months have more hot days, some have more rainy days).
    ii.   The differences in relative temperature over the course of a day (e.g., between early morning and the afternoon, between one day and another) are directly related to the time of day.
	Ch-10

ESS3.B: Natural Hazards • Some kinds of severe weather are more likely than others in a given region. Weather scientists forecast severe weather so that the communities can prepare for and respond to these events.	Ch-10
ETS1.A: Defining and Delimiting an Engineering Problem 1. Asking questions, making observations, and gathering information are helpful in thinking about problems. i. Students formulate questions about local severe weather, the answers to which would clarify how weather forecasting can help people avoid the most serious impacts of severe weather events. 2 Identifying the scientific nature of the question	Ch-10
3 Obtaining information Students collect information (e.g., from questions, grade appropriate texts, media) about local severe weather warnings (e.g., tornado alerts, hurricane warnings, major thunderstorm warnings, winter storm warnings, severe drought alerts, heat wave alerts), including that:	Ch-10

i. There are patterns related to local severe weather that can be observed (e.g., certain types of severe weather happen more in certain places). ii. Weather patterns (e.g., some events are more likely in certain regions) help scientists predict severe weather before it happens. iii. Severe weather warnings are used to communicate predictions about severe weather. iv. Weather forecasting can help people plan for, and respond to, specific types of local weather (e.g., responses: stay indoors during severe weather, go to cooling centers during heat waves; preparations: evacuate coastal areas before a hurricane, cover windows before storms).	
ETS1.A: Defining and Delimiting Engineering Problems • A situation that people want to change or create can be approached as a problem to be solved through engineering. • Asking questions, making observations, and gathering information are helpful in thinking about problems. • Before beginning to design a solution, it is important to clearly understand the problem. Students use the information they have gathered, including the answers to their questions, observations they have made, and scientific information, to describe* the situation people want to change in terms of a simple problem that can be solved with the development of a new or improved object or tool.	Ch-16
K-PS2-1. Plan and conduct an investigation to compare the effects of different strengths or different directions of pushes and pulls on the motion of an object. Examples of pushes or pulls could include a string attached to an object being pulled, a person pushing an object, a person stopping a rolling ball, and two objects colliding and pushing on each other.] [Assessment Boundary: Assessment is limited to different relative strengths or different directions, but not both at the same time. Assessment does not include non-contact pushes or pulls such as those produced by magnets.]	Ch-7,8
K-PS2-2. Analyze data to determine if a design solution works as intended to change the speed or direction of an object with a push or a pull.* [Clarification Statement: Examples of problems requiring a solution could include having a marble or other object move a certain distance, follow a particular path, and knock down other objects. Examples of solutions could include tools such as a ramp	Ch-8

to increase the speed of the object and a structure that would cause an object such as a marble or ball to turn.] **K-ESS2-1.** **Use and share observations of local weather conditions to describe patterns over time.** [Clarification Statement: Examples of qualitative observations could include descriptions of the weather (such as sunny, cloudy, rainy, and warm); examples of quantitative observations could include numbers of sunny, windy, and rainy days in a month. Examples of patterns could include that it is usually cooler in the morning than in the afternoon and the number of sunny days versus cloudy days in different months.]	
K-2-ETS1-3. Analyze data from tests of two objects designed to solve the same problem to compare the strengths and weaknesses of how each performs. Two balls of the same size collide and change direction. A cart pulled across a floor moves quicker with a strong pull than with a weak pull.	Ch-8
K-PS2-1 Motion and Stability: Forces and Interactions **Disciplinary Core Ideas**	Ch-7
PS2.A: Forces and Motion • Pushes and pulls can have different strengths and directions. • Pushing or pulling on an object can change the speed or direction of its motion and can start or stop it.	Ch-8
PS2.B: Types of Interactions • When objects touch or collide, they push on one another and can change motion.	Ch-8

PS3.C: Relationship Between Energy and Forces
• A bigger push or pull makes things speed up or slow down more quickly.
 	
Identifying the phenomenon to be investigated
   a. With guidance, students collaboratively identify the phenomenon under investigation, which includes the following idea: the effect caused by different strengths and directions of pushes and pulls on the motion of an object.
   b. With guidance, students collaboratively identify the purpose of the investigation, which includes gathering evidence to support or refute student ideas about causes
	Ch-6,8

of the phenomenon by comparing the effects of different strengths of pushes and pulls on the motion of an object.
 	
Identifying the evidence to address this purpose of the investigation
    a. With guidance, students collaboratively develop an investigation plan to investigate the relationship between the strength and direction of pushes and pulls and the motion of an object (i.e., qualitative measures or expressions of strength and <u>direction;</u> e.g., harder, softer, descriptions* of "which way").
    b. Students describe* how the observations they make connect to the purpose of the investigation, including how the observations of the effects on object motion allow causal relationships between pushes and pulls and object motion to be determined
    c. Students predict the effect of the push of pull on the motion of the object, based on prior experiences.
	Ch-8

3   Planning the investigation
    a. In the collaboratively developed investigation plan, students describe*:
          i. The object whose motion will be investigated.
          ii. What will be in contact with the object to cause the push or pull.
          iii. The relative strengths of the push or pull that will be applied to the object to start or stop its motion or change its speed.
          iv. The relative directions of the push or pull that will be applied to the object.
          v. How the motion of the object will be observed and recorded.
          vi. How the push or pull will be applied to vary strength or direction.
	Ch-8

PS2.A: Forces and Motion • Pushes and pulls can have different strengths and directions. • Pushing or pulling on an object can change the speed or direction of its motion and can start or stop it.	Ch-6,7,8
ETS1.A: Defining Engineering Problems • A situation that people want to change or create can be approached as a problem to be solved through engineering. Such problems may have many acceptable solutions. a. With guidance, students organize given information using graphical or visual displays (e.g., pictures, pictographs,	Ch-8

drawings, written observations, tables, charts). The given information students organize includes: ii. The relative speed or direction of the object before a push or pull is applied (i.e., qualitative measures and expressions of speed and <u>direction</u>; e.g., faster, slower, descriptions* of "which way"). ii. The relative speed or direction of the object after a push or pull is applied. iii. How the relative strength of a push or pull affects the speed or direction of an object (i.e., qualitative measures or expressions of <u>strength</u>; e.g., harder,	Ch-8
K-ESS2-1 Earth's Systems	Ch-13

Made in the USA
Middletown, DE
27 April 2022